EFFECTIVE COMMUNICATION AT WORK

Say what you mean
and get what you want

EFFECTIVE COMMUNICATION AT WORK

Say what you mean
and get what you want

Written by Virginie De Lutis
Translated by Emma Lunt

COMMUNICATING EFFECTIVELY AT WORK

- **Issue:** how can I develop clear and healthy communication at work?
- **Uses:** good communication at work is necessary to motivate and improve the efficiency of employees, resolve conflicts and maintain healthy professional relationships.
- **Professional context:** professional relationships, professional communication, human resources.
- **FAQs:**
  - What things do I need to pay attention to when I communicate with my colleagues?
  - What types of communication are found in the office?
  - How should I communicate with my manager?
  - How can I make my meetings effective?
  - How do I avoid rumours and power games?
  - What is the purpose of evaluations and feedback?
  - Should I communicate differently if I am a woman?
  - How can I re-establish communication within my team?

Communication is essential for a company to function well, yet it can be the source of misunderstandings or even conflicts, and cause an atmosphere that is damaging to the wellbeing and effectiveness of employees. Rumours, innuendos and unsaid things are all situations we are likely to encounter over the course of our professional lives, so we should take a close interest in this phenomenon.

But how do we go about encouraging healthier and more effective conversations that respect and motivate employees? Whereas previous models overwhelmed the people involved with information without taking the human aspect into account, today's companies are developing an increasing number of strategies that promote and nurture tolerant, useful and close communication. Nevertheless, establishing this kind of process takes time and must respect certain principles. In 50 minutes, this guide will put into perspective the different aspects of all internal communication, as well as the obstacles that you may encounter within the company. It will also offer you solutions to successfully transmit clear and effective messages in order to improve your professional relationships.

HOW TO BE A GREAT COMMUNICATOR AT WORK: THE BASICS

THE PRINCIPLES OF COMMUNICATION

The key components of communication

All communication involves three main components: an emitter, a message and a receiver. Taking this classic outline as our starting point, we will examine the essential characteristics of exchanges between colleagues, teams and managers.

The emitter Produces the message consciously or subconsciously:	The message Can be in different forms depending on the situation. It can be:	The receiver Receives the message. They can react in many different ways:
• by addressing the other person directly; • by transmitting messages through their emotions, body language, etc.	• a solely verbal message; • a verbal message accompanied by a nonverbal message. The two can contradict each other; • a nonverbal message, meaning an attitude that they have either consciously adopted or not, that communicates without emitting any sound (silence is an aspect of communication).	• they may take on board the information that they have received; • they may react to the speech; • they may ignore the message or push it to one side without even acknowledging it.

The components given as examples above are not exhaustive but can remind you of colleagues or situations that you have experienced. In order for your messages to be heard and understood, speaking is not enough: you must communicate, which means connecting with the other person. During these interpersonal exchanges, which are also called "transactions" by Eric Berne (American psychiatrist, founder of transactional analysis, 1910-1970), we create interchangeable roles. According to this specialist, we all answer to three ego-states - the Parent, Adult and Child states – and juggle between them based on our exchanges and the position that the other person adopts. Furthermore, speakers can change their role during a conversation, depending on their emotions and the subject being raised.

Nonverbal communication

The success of our communication does not only depend on words (written or spoken): nonverbal language also plays a significant part. According to Albert Mehrabian (psychology professor, born in 1939), it even seems that this latter type is the most communicative:

Types of language

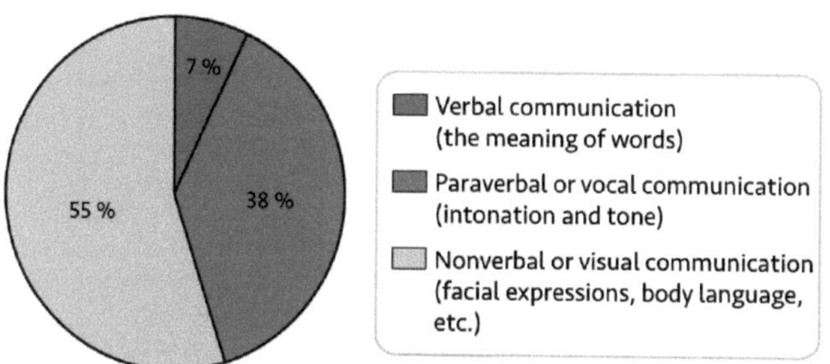

You must be aware of the components that make up nonverbal language in order to control the information that you transmit.

Gestures and behaviours	Voice	Scents
The way you walk, your posture and your facial expressions are all elements that portray who you are and what you feel. In this way, a lack of behaviours and gestures is a sign of communication. A well-known NLP (neuro-linguistic programming) technique involves skilfully imitating the other person's behaviour in order to create immediate proximity.	The tone of your voice and your delivery form a significant part of your nonverbal language. It is extremely important to achieve congruence between these factors, your attitude and the message you are emitting. Record yourself during a conversation with a friend, as this will give you a first impression of what you are transmitting when you speak, beyond just words.	In her studies, Martha McClintock, an American psychologist (born in 1947) explains that we emit variable smells according to our feelings (stress, sadness, anger, etc.) and that we are attracted by people who has a similar olfactory profile as our own. The olfactory signals that our bodies send out correspond to our emotions.

Suggested behaviours	Behaviours to avoid
• Look the other person in the eye in order to maintain visual contact • Have a firm handshake • Relax your face and smile • Respect the other person's space and do not get too close • Take care of your appearance (clothing, smell, etc.)	• Rubbing your neck or your hands together shows doubt or insecurity • Saying "yes" while shaking your head "no" suggests a contradiction in your ideas • Leaning back in your chair indicates that you are withdrawing from the conversation • Folding your arms closes you off to any discussion • Arching your back and leaning forwards shows a lack of self-confidence • Gesticulating in any way and playing with your hair

IMAGE COACHING

Image coaching is a fashionable practice, notably thanks to makeover television programmes. It helps you to galvanise your appearance and assert yourself by choosing an outfit that suits your body type, your complexion and your personality. The image that you portray is as important as what you say. Feeling happy in your body will help you to be confident in yourself, which will lead to a certain ease when you express yourself.

Verbal communication

Even if it only represents 7% of our communication, verbal language is the basis of the Adult's information, if we use Berne's model. By depending on objective information, your communication will be clearer. To converse effectively, pay attention to the following tips:

- Communicating is about being committed and getting involved. Express yourself by starting your sentences with "I": "I think", "I suggest", "I propose", etc. You will thus express your feelings and ideas without incriminating others or relying on rumours. For example, say "I am overwhelmed" rather than "You do not pay attention to my workload".
- If you do not understand something, ask for clarification immediately rather than allowing doubts or misunderstandings to linger.
- The most advanced technology does not necessarily improve communication. You should therefore be careful with your emails and professional writing when you communicate. Use the appropriate greetings, be brief and precise, etc.
- Impose yourself when it is necessary. If somebody cuts you off, do not hesitate to ask them why they are interrupting you and point out to them that you were in the middle of speaking.
- Similarly, when somebody addresses you, listen attentively without cutting them off and stay focused.
- Adapt your vocabulary so that the person you are speaking to understands your words.

COMMUNICATION AT WORK

Why does it deserve our attention?

Good internal communication is the basis for all success at work. Among other things, it serves to:

- ensure that objectives and instructions are understood;
- unite employees on a project;
- get employees involved and participating in the company's culture;
- motivate employees;
- resolve conflicts;
- ensure balanced and pleasant relationships;
- create a friendly atmosphere.

Formal communication

Formal communication is used for all official exchanges among individuals in a company. These can be:

- Professional writings, such as emails, notices or meeting reports which, with time and new technologies, can vary widely. We can thus see the forward-looking nature of companies that favour electronic messages over paper communications. Others, however, have not yet invested in a computer system and prefer printed versions.
- Oral exchanges such as meetings, feedback sessions and interviews.

Formal communication can take several forms:

Type of formal communication		Flow of information
Descending or hierarchical	M ⟶ E	From management to the employees
Ascending or salary	M ⟵ E	From the employees to management
Lateral or horizontal	E_1 ⟷ E_2	An exchange between employees at the same level or within structures without a hierarchy

THE MANAGER AS A CONDUCTOR

A new management method recently appeared within companies: MBWA (Management By Wandering Around). Rather than focusing on reports and meetings, the manager takes the time to talk to their team members and to get closer to their everyday life at work. This closeness helps them to ensure their team's compliance with instructions and their understanding of decisions, to ensure internal communication tools are working well and identify aspects that could be improved, to take note of their employees' opinions, and also to congratulate and motivate their team. By going to meet them and listening to them, the manager indirectly reinforces the effectiveness of formal communication.

The format and objective of each of these exchanges are determined by the emitter of the message according to the ideas seen above. For example, a boss who is not often available will primarily communicate through email by going through managers who relay instructions or by directly addressing their employees to maintain contact with them. Once again, the manner in which information is spread depends on the work philosophy and culture of the company.

Informal communication

Informal communication is used in all non-official exchanges, which take place at work but are not necessarily about professional problems. This kind of communication includes discussions around the coffee machine, between two offices, during a lunch or cigarette break, etc. Some managers are wary of this type of communication, as it is spontaneous, does not follow norms and often delivers unverified information (rumours, gossip, etc.) that can lead to conflicts and awkwardness. Just like formal communication, it can take place through different means, written (email, Post-it) or oral, and has many advantages:

- It provides a status and satisfies the need to be recognised and to belong to a group;
- it promotes the sharing of social and cultural values within a collective;
- it encourages collaboration by creating connections between employees.

There are no rules to follow or a magical user guide. Moreover, you must respect the principles of politeness in order to develop and maintain healthy and productive professional relationships.

ADAPT YOUR BEHAVIOUR

Whatever the type of communication, the behaviours that we adopt are a determining factor and influence how the exchange plays out. According to Eric Berne, there are three ego-states, which correspond to specific behaviours:

- **(P) the Parent** who imitates the parental figure, which is both authoritative and welcoming;
- **(A) the Adult** who is concerned by the factual aspect of things, logical and rational information, and the here and now;
- **(C) the Child** who refers to our experiences and memories of childhood.

The following table will help you to understand the complexity of these states.

Ego-states	Descriptions	Examples
P Normative or critical	Represents the law. Acts as a protector and educator. Tends to judge and sanction.	"You are late, it is unacceptable!"
P Nurturing or a rescuer	Offers permission and encouragement. Empathetic and warm. Tends to be overprotective.	"You should take care of yourself."
A	Analyses facts. Objective, rational and fair. Tends to resolve and avoid conflicts.	"What time is the meeting?"
E Free and spontaneous	Expresses basic needs and emotions spontaneously.	"I love your blouse, I want one like that."
E Adapted (rebellious or submissive)	Expresses themselves as a reaction to the behaviour of others.	"I am not going to do it!" "It was not my fault."

In order to have constructive and appropriate exchanges within the company, transactions (or exchanges) absolutely must be complementary, meaning Adult to Adult or Parent to Child.

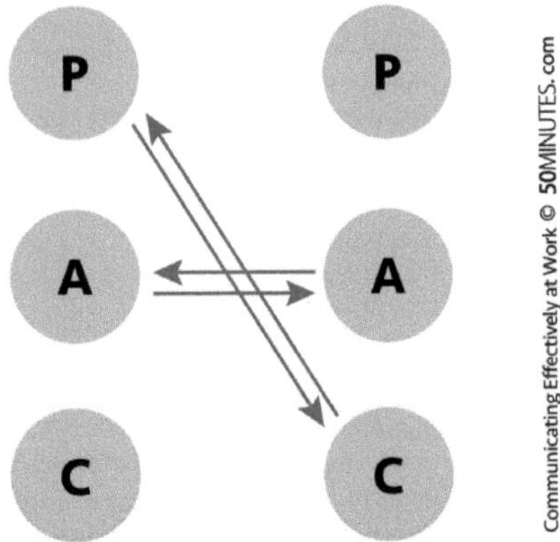

Beware that if your transactions cross over, this can cause conflicts.

> **For example:**
> - "What time is he arriving?" (Adult)
> - "You should know!" (Parent)

In this type of transaction, the balance is not respected as one of the two speakers is treated like a child, while they have positioned themselves as an adult as our outline below shows:

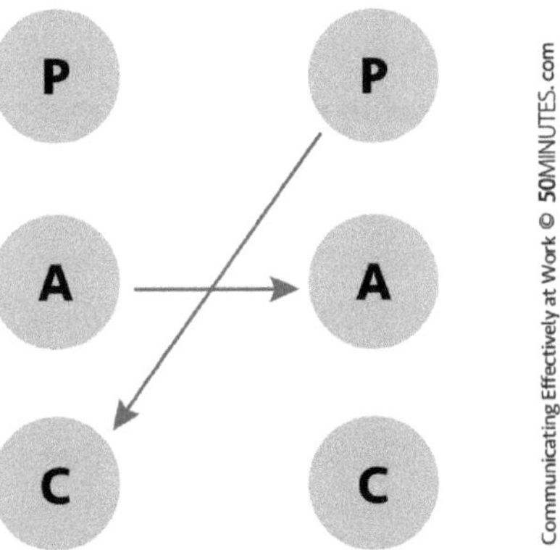

> **Example response in an Adult-Adult exchange**
> "He arrives at 10:30. It irritates me that you do not remember this sort of information, as it seems to me that you are not taking this meeting seriously." (Adult)

Pay attention to this type of discrepancy, as power games often take place without the participants' knowledge. They harm the company's productivity and cause resentment within the team. When you converse with your colleagues or superiors, all your communication reveals your ego-state.

Transactional analysis offers good solutions to free yourself from unpleasant power games, by inviting you to adopt the most appropriate state depending on the situation. Thus, if you behave like a "normative Parent" with everybody, it is quite logical that this will create tensions among colleagues. If you want to get results from your employees, you should act as an "Adult" by providing factual instructions (when, where, who, etc.). If you wish to regard your colleagues in a professional manner (therefore as an Adult), act in this way. For some informal exchanges, where being welcoming (Parent) is appropriate, act more empathetically and warmly in your words and attitude. For example, if your employee is very unmotivated at work, but does not admit it, rather than accepting their denial or forcing them to speak, concentrate on your objective: to see things more clearly in order to improve the professional situation. In order to do this, put yourself in the state that seems suitable. Normative authoritative Parent? Nurturing and rational Parent? Maybe you should try to be a nurturing, welcoming and warm Parent.

Examples situations

Situation	Good reaction	Bad reaction
"I have been waiting for your report since this morning, is it finished yet?" (Normative parent)	"I am just finishing it now." (Adult)	"If only you would stop disturbing me, I would be able to finish it." (Rebellious child)
"I am never going to manage to finish this report on time." (Submissive child)	"But you are our best asset on the project." (Nurturing parent)	"You are right, it is going to be very complicated" (Submissive child)
"Come on, it is time for a coffee break." (Free child)	"Great, I'll join you." (Free child) "I am not going to be able to, I have to finish this file for the meeting tomorrow." (Adult)	"You never work!" (Normative parent)

TOP TIPS

- **Express yourself using the pronoun "I".** You will thus show your involvement in the conversation and will stand up for your positions. Choose the positive form over the negative. For example, say "Do you remember that we have a meeting tomorrow?" rather than "You haven't forgotten our meeting tomorrow morning, have you?".
- **Adopt welcoming body language** in order to put the other person at ease. Eliminate as much as possible any behavioural tics that would give away your nervousness, unease or anger (gesticulating nervously, hiding your hands in your pockets, biting your nails, etc.). The other person will then focus on your words and not on your body language.
- **Control your emotions.** Whatever the situation (negative feedback, an unpleasant remark from a colleague, etc.), do not show yourself to be too aggressive or defensive, as this will not lead to any positive solution. Take a step back, try to understand the other person and, if necessary, calmly explain what is bothering you in order to ease the tension.
- **Establish trusting relationships** around you. Act with kindness to encourage your colleagues to do the same. Likewise, denounce and condemn any abusive, sexist, racist or humiliating behaviour. These behaviours are unacceptable within any community and can lead to the resignation, and even burnout, of some employees.
- **Adapt yourself to the other person.** Pay attention to their verbal and body language. If they are tactile,

hug them; if they are visual, illustrate your speech with the help of concrete examples; if they are more auditory, choose oral communication over written; etc. Furthermore, adjust your way of expressing yourself according to whether you are addressing your manager or a direct colleague.

- **Organise internal open door days,** in order to encourage exchanges and to reinforce collaboration between departments. Introduce your colleagues to the internal functioning so that everybody is aware of the processes and roles of each service. This will considerably reduce misunderstandings and discrepancies.
- **Develop an internal network.** The internal network represents a bank of information and knowledge that is interesting and beneficial for the whole company. It invites employees to discuss specific aspects (rather than general content that nobody consults) from time to time. For example, a department could create a journal describing their daily activities, which would make the work of the department in charge of taking over the project in the medium to long term much easier. You can also create a social network for the company. Based on classic social networking models, it offers employees the chance to exchange, publish information or quickly communicate with each other. This will reinforce their cohesion.
- **Set specific times for communicating** so as to not disturb or break the concentration of the people to whom you are talking at all hours of the day. Organise information meetings and interviews if you need time with a particular person. Do not forget to let them know early enough by indicating what it is about. If you only

have to explain a particular detail, try to talk over coffee or during the lunch break.

- **Choose between collective or one-on-one meetings** depending on the type of information to be delivered. If you have to remind an employee of the rules following inappropriate behaviour, there is no point involving the whole company. Following collective meetings, make a report of the decisions made available to inform those who are interested (present or absent).
- **Establish a relaxation space** to encourage informal exchanges. This will improve professional relationships and the atmosphere of your team. Shorter or informal meetings can also take place there.

ALTRUISTIC RELATIONSHIPS

Matthieu Ricard, a doctor in biology who converted to Buddhism, cites altruism as a success factor at work. According to him, man naturally turns to others and not to himself. Similarly, statistics by the OECD (Organisation for Economic Co-operation and Development) determine that the number one criterion for happiness is by far the quality of relationships. Their research reveals that good communication comes with altruism and good interactions with colleagues. According to Ricard, practicing meditation could become a teambuilding tool, as it encourages lasting cooperation and harmony and promotes the development of a healthy and kind environment. Nowadays, some companies create relaxation spaces and invite their employees to meditate there alone or in groups in order to improve their relationships and thus their communication.

FAQS

WHAT THINGS DO I NEED TO PAY ATTENTION TO WHEN I COMMUNICATE WITH MY COLLEAGUES?

There are many things that you should keep in mind: your gestures, your behaviour, your appearance, the tone of your voice and the words that you use. By assembling these things in a harmonious way, you will transmit clear and direct messages. Furthermore, pay attention to the other person when they speak to you, look them in the eyes and listen to them. Focus on what they are saying and their body language. If you do not understand something, ask for further explanation. If you feel that an emotion is concealed behind their words, speak about it in a kind way: the goal here is not to play the psychologist, but rather to promote frank and honest communication between colleagues.

WHAT TYPES OF COMMUNICATION ARE FOUND IN THE OFFICE?

The types of communication and methods used vary depending on the size of the organisation in which you work and the culture of your company. Nonetheless, it is generally necessary to master IT, as emails, the intranet and videoconferences are the most common communication tools. Of course, there is also verbal and oral communication which is used in meetings and interviews and for feedback, without forgetting the informal exchanges around the coffee machine.

HOW SHOULD I COMMUNICATE WITH MY MANAGER?

According to the philosophy and internal functioning of the company, you may never come into contact with the top manager. Consequently, your superior will be a manager who themselves meets the standards of the internal policy of your organisation. If you want to promote collaboration, enquire about this at the interview stage and ask who your manager will be so that the roles are clearly established. During every exchange, let your manager express themselves using the communication method and tone that they prefer (familiar, cold, direct, etc.) and adapt yourself to their attitude. As a precaution, use formal language with them and maintain some professional distance, at least until you know them better.

HOW CAN I MAKE MY MEETINGS EFFECTIVE?

Do not confirm your attendance at a meeting if you do not know what is on the agenda. Ask for further information about the topic and the issue. You will thus arrive prepared or, if necessary, can warn of your absence. If all employees are required to attend but you feel, as is often the case, that it is a waste of time, suggest one-on-one meetings or meetings with the people who are directly affected. This will be more effective and motivating for everyone.

HOW DO I AVOID RUMOURS AND POWER GAMES?

Rumours can reveal dysfunctions within the organisation. Internal communication aims to avoid these by maintaining contact with employees and by seeking to find what is feeding their fears, gossip or frustrations. To help you to identify problems, analyse the four following points in your organisation:

- the quality of collaboration, i.e. listening, respect for the manager, oral expression and debate;
- engagement, namely a welcoming environment, cohesion within the team, eliminating the fear of comparison;
- power management; when handled in a measured way, a manager's leadership does not tread on teams;
- conflict resolution, meaning perceiving conflict as a productive moment, distinguishing the person from the topic behind discussed, finding solutions or encouraging compromise.

Frank and effective communication cannot exist in an unkind environment where everybody fears the things that are left unsaid and interpersonal tensions. In an atmosphere where these risks are diminished, and where the team's maturity enables everybody to make the most of their potential (by making mistakes, asking questions, looking for contradictions in debate to improve their work, etc.), the organisation finds a productive solidarity among its employees, which is fed by their intelligence.

WHAT IS THE PURPOSE OF EVALUATIONS AND FEEDBACK?

Evaluations and feedback represent privileged times that are used to by managers to interact with their subordinates, or vice versa. Therefore, do not hesitate to ask about the topics that will be dealt with in order to prepare for them. Evaluations offer a chance to talk about aspirations, assessments and ideas, but also any difficulties encountered. If you are called for this type of meeting, prepare a file with your suggestions in a professional manner, so that you can inform your superiors of them. During a feedback meeting, these superiors will give you feedback on your skills and behaviours. Listen calmly and do not take the remarks as criticism, but as opportunities to improve.

SHOULD I COMMUNICATE DIFFERENTLY IF I AM A WOMAN?

Some men do not hesitate to belittle women by continuing to believe untrue things (women are emotional, weaker, cannot handle stress as well, etc.) and sometimes go so far as to make unkind remarks. To reinforce your self-confidence as a woman, be inspired by the techniques of specialists, such as Amy Cuddy's power poses, which act on the subconscious. Mock these types of sexist comments and do not hesitate to contact representative bodies if no sanction or decision is made to put a stop to these harmful actions. Social partners (trade unions, work committees, etc.) can suggest appropriate measures to re-establish a calm and civilised atmosphere within communication at work.

During a TED Talk entitled "Your Body Language Shapes Who You Are", American psychologist Amy Cuddy explains that changing our posture has a positive impact on others' perception of us, but especially on the perception we have of ourselves. After doing simple experiments for two minutes on behaviours to adopt, Cuddy shows that body language has an effect on the testosterone levels, on tolerance to risk and on cortisol levels. These hormonal changes control the brain and drive us to react with a feeling of power or stress. Cuddy therefore suggests imitating poses that put us in a strong position and feed our self-confidence: hands on your hips, chest puffed out, back straight, etc. Apply this advice as often as possible by adopting these poses or those of self-assured colleagues until you feel more confident.

HOW CAN I RE-ESTABLISH COMMUNICATION WITHIN MY TEAM?

Teambuilding is an effective solution for re-establishing healthy communication at work. To make it relevant, organise it around subjects related to your issue (conflict resolution, group dynamic, communication within the team, etc.). Call on an organiser from outside the organisation so that everybody, including the manager, can benefit from the workshop. What matters here is that the person who plays the role of leader in the group sets an example and that everybody in the organisation takes part in the process.

OVER TO YOU

Stand in front of the mirror and give your impression of:

- your outfit;
- the way you say hello;
- the tone of your voice.

Now think about one of your colleagues who is confident and at ease and analyse the differences between their attitude and yours. Is their way of speaking in accordance with their style and personality? Is it soft, fast, effective, understandable? As for you, is your expression consistent with your temperament? Correct these aspects based on your answers.

RE-ESTABLISH TRUST IN YOUR TEAM

If you feel that power games or unsaid things are affecting the atmosphere in your team and slowing down the organisation's projects, study the situation. Ask yourself the following questions to understand the origin of these conflicts. Try to resolve them internally or with the help of a coach during a team-building session.

- How do the games play out? Are the people involved always the same? Do they play the same roles?
- Has somebody already spoken to them about their behaviour? Have you done it personally?

- What behaviour do you notice most often? How can you explain to the individual concerned that their behaviour is harmful? ("Why do you constantly interrupt me?", "Why are you so aggressive when you express yourself? It affects the team.", etc.).
- Position those involved within the table of ego-states: Parent (nurturing or normative), Adult, Child (submissive, rebellious or spontaneous). What information stands out from this?

FURTHER READING

BIBLIOGRAPHY

- Bastianutti, J. and Petitbon, F. (2015) *La proximité, une stratégie!* Paris: Dunod.
- D'Almeida, N. and Libaert, T. (2010) *La communication interne des entreprises.* Paris: Dunod.
- Duterne, C. (2002) *La communication interne en entreprise.* Brussels: De Boeck.
- Ghiulamila, J. and Levet, P. (2007) *Les hommes, les femmes et les entreprises: vers quelle égalité?* Paris: Éditions L'Harmattan.
- Goldstein, M. and Read, P. (2009) *Games At Work: How to Recognize and Reduce Office Politics.* San Francisco: Jossey-Bass.
- Nutra News. (2000) *Les pheromones, des messagers biochimiques qui agissent sur les comportements sexuel et social.* [Online]. [Accessed 8 August 2015]. Available from: <http://www.nutranews.org/sujet.pl?id=684>
- Terrier, C. (2013) L'analyse transactionelle. *Cterrier. com.* [Online]. [Accessed 9 August 2015]. Available from: <http://www.cterrier.com/cours/communication/32_analyse_transactionnelle.pdf>
- Tonnelé, A. (2015) *La bible du team-building. 55 fiches pour développer la performance des équipes.* Paris: Eyrolles.

ADDITIONAL SOURCES

- Berne, E. (1969) *Games People Play*. New York: Vintage.
- Krotov, V. (2016) *Mindful Written Communication: Master the Most Fundamental Principles of Effective Written Communication in Less Than One Hour*. London: Enso Text.

Videos

- *Dare to Disagree*. (2012) [Video]. Margaret Heferman. Available from: <http://www.ted.com/talks/margaret_heff ernan_dare_to_disagree>
- *How to Let Altruism Be Your Guide*. (2014) [Video]. Matthieu Ricard. Available from: <http://www.ted.com/talks/matthieu_ricard_how_to_let_altruism_be_your_guide>
- *Le visage décrypté*. (2011) [Video]. Available from: < http://www.arte.tv/guide/fr/043564-000/le-visage-decrypte>
- *Les odeurs corporelles: un moyen de communication?* (2004) [Video]. Available from: <https://www.youtube.com/watch?v=PZQJFcbF_ig>
- *Non verbal: les gestes qui tuent votre crédibilité*. (2014) [Video]. Available from: <https://www.youtube.com/watch?v=k-s_R4yZEuY>
- *Why Good Leaders Make You Feel Safe*. (2014) [Video]. Simon Snek. Available from: <http://www.ted.com/talks/simon_sinek_why_good_leaders_make_you_feel_safe>

- *Why Work Doesn't Happen at Work.* (2010) [Video]. Jason Fried. Available from: <http://www.ted.com/talks/jason_fried_why_work_doesn_t_happen_at_work>
- *Your Body Language Shapes Who You Are.* (2012) [Video]. Amy Cuddy. Available from: <http://www.ted.com/talks/amy_cuddy_your_body_language_shapes_who_you_are>